Carving Traditional
Woodspirits
with Tom Wolfe

77 Lower Valley Road, Atglen, PA 19310

Text written with and photography by Douglas Congdon-Martin

Contents

Designed by Bonnie Hensley

Printed in the United States of America.
ISBN: 0-88740-538-x

Published by Schiffer Publishing, Ltd.
77 Lower Valley Road
Atglen, PA 19310
Please write for a free catalog.
This book may be purchased from the publisher.
Please include $2.95 postage.
Try your bookstore first.

We are interested in hearing from authors
with book ideas on related subjects.

Introduction

Woodspirits have a long and noble history. They are found in different forms in almost every culture on the earth. From Greek myths, to fairy tales, to the stories of American mountain people, the Woodspirit is a vivid and powerful character.

The Woodspirits we carve in this book resemble those that traditionally have been carved in Bavaria for hundreds of years. The carving schools in the Black Forest still teach ways to carve this type of figure. Their methods, however, differ quite significantly from mine.

From the response to the first book of *Woodspirits and Walking Sticks*, it is clear that these figures are enchanting still. They offer the wood carver the opportunity to be creative and to let the wood take on unique shapes. This is quite different from carving from a pattern and presents the carver with both challenge and opportunity.

This project is carved from a segment of white pine, although other woods may also be used. I have chosen to paint it, but, as you can see in the gallery, Woodspirits are also beautiful in natural finishes.

As always I hope you enjoy carving and living with the Woodspirits!

Carving the Woodspirit

As a work surface for my woodspirits I use a piece of wood attached with countersunk screws to a 360 degree hydraulic hold down. The wood is kind to my tools when I make mistakes. The hydraulic hold down will withstand substantial blows without moving. The piece is attached to the wood through the back with screws.

The hold down is attached to a black custom-made expansion piece that is attached to a Ritter dentist's chair base. The base is on locking wheels, though if you work in a permanent place, you are better off without them.

Though it is not easy to find the dentist chair base is excellent for carving. It pumps up and down hydraulically, has a release, and swivels 360 degrees with a lock to hold its position. If I had had this thirty years ago I could have done 10,000 more carvings by now.

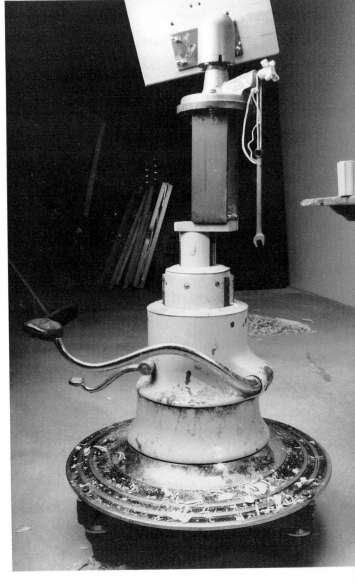

White pine is great for these woodspirits because all the limbs emerge at the same circle of the trunk.

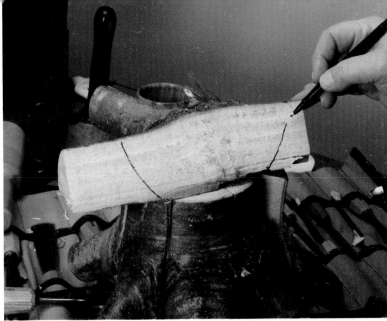

After visualizing the size of the hat band, I would saw along these lines to get the general shape of the face.

This means you can get several blanks from one segment of a tree.

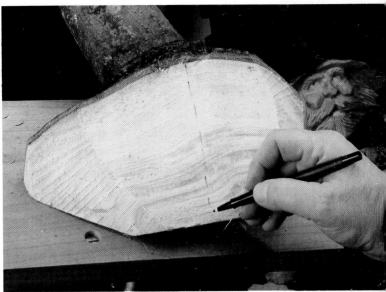

Mark the center line based on the hat.

Split the log apart with a band saw, for smaller ones like this, or a chain saw for bigger pieces. If you don't have a band saw, you can split the wood by hand.

Use a large half-round gouge to come in under the brim of the hat. Cut from the center out. The grain goes across the piece and around the branch, so working from the center makes things go much more smoothly.

Continue around the side.

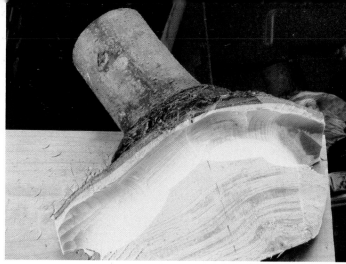

The brim emerges.

This brings the hat over the hair line.

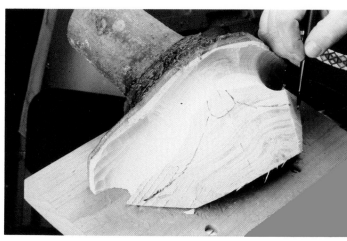

Draw in the line of the nose and moustache. The moustache will sweep back around the side.

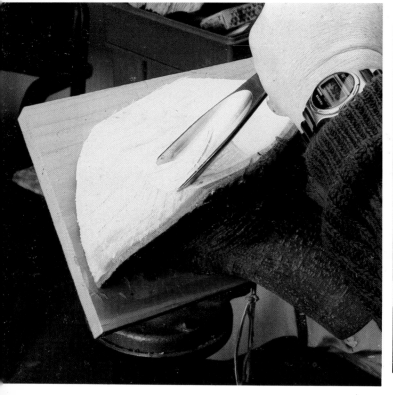

Turn the piece over and continue on the other side.

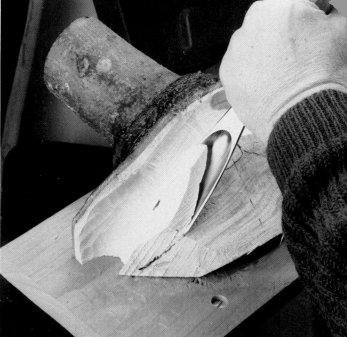

Follow the line of the moustache with the bottom edge of the chisel.

The result.

Come down the side of the face, but only back to the hairline.

Do the same thing on the other side.

The result.

I want the face to be about as wide as the crown of the hat so it looks natural. Here it is marked.

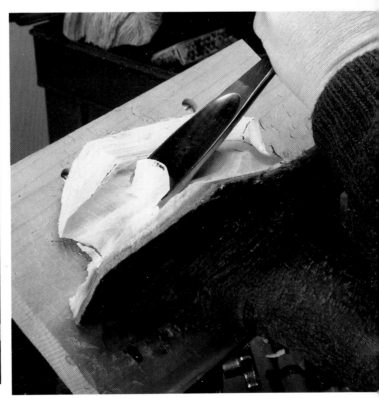

Repeat on the other side.

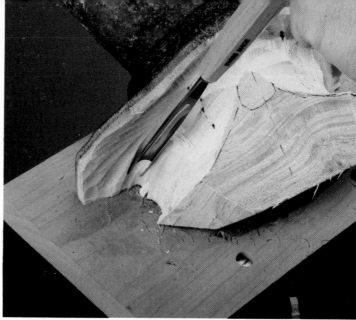

Move to a smaller half-round chisel go up under the brim a little bit, making it look like the brim is going over his eyes.

The final cut is over and down and is the line where the brim meets the hair.

Carry the lines of the brim out to the side.

Repeat on the other side.

Work your way back to the hairline on the side.

The brim.

With the larger gouge, start at the middle and carve out to the edge to define the eye socket.

Progress.

Two or three passes should get you as deep as you want.

Cut a stop in the end of the nose using a gouge with a curve that nearly matches the curve of the nose and driving it straight in. You don't want to go too far, only an 1/8th inch or so at first. This creates a stop.

Repeat on the other side.

Use a flatter gouge to cut back to the nose stop along the moustache line.

Continue all across the bottom of the nose.

Deepen again.

Go back and deepen the nose stop. Go about a quarter of an inch. You don't want to break off the nose. This deepening will cut off the chips created in the previous step.

Trim across the front of the moustache to make it wider, using a flatter gouge.

Trim under the nose again.

Continue down the mouth.

Come across the bridge of the nose with a half-round gouge...

From the eyebrow notch come down around the underside of the eyebrow...

and bring the line around into the eye socket.

and continue a groove across to the temple area.

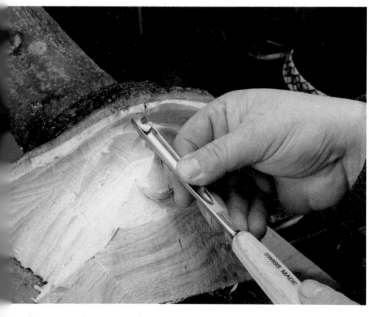

Separate between the eyebrows.

Visualize or draw the line between the moustache and the cheek.

With a wide gouge go straight in, creating a line of the cheek.

Progress. Note the line of the cheek and the beginnings of the moustache.

Turn the chisel and use a corner to make a stop beside the nostril.

With a skew go straight in beside the nostril to create a good, deep cut.

With the same chisel come back to the cheek from below and cut out a slice.

Come back toward this cut at a slight angle.

A cut up from the bottom will take out the chip.

Repeat on the other side.

The nose is starting to emerge.

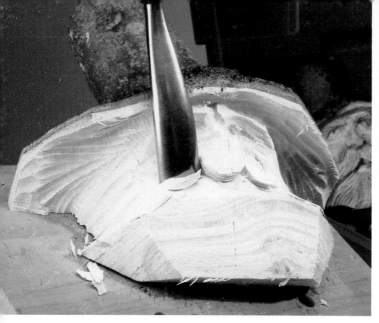

With the cup side against the face come over the cheek and round it off.

At the temple reverse the gouge so the cup is away from the face.

This is the result.

Come back with the flat chisel and clean up the chips.

Continue the line around the side.

At the temple first cut along the face under the brim.

Then cut along the temple line to clean out the chip.

The upper face is taking shape.

The result.

With a smaller chisel come around the outside of the eye, bringing the eye line back to the temple. Repeat on the other side.

Do the other side in the same way.

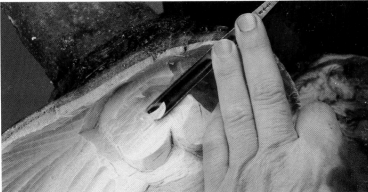

The eyesocket needed to be deepened a little bit, so I used the same gouge to clean it out. Use strokes going from the nose out.

With a half round gouge, hold the cup away from the nose and cut in under the nostril.

At the end, the chip will pop right off.

Going across the grain like this, they just fall right out.

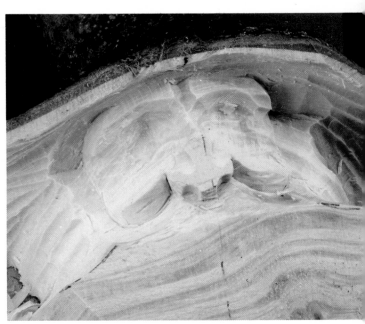

Repeat on the other side. This gives the basic shape to the nostrils.

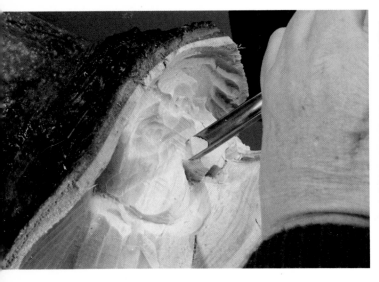

With the same gouge go over the top line of the nostril.

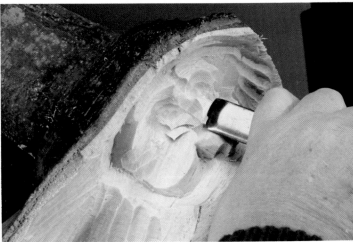

Use a pretty flat gouge with the cup side down to shape the nose.

With the cup side out begin to shape the nostril.

Come over the nostril with the gouge to give it more definition.

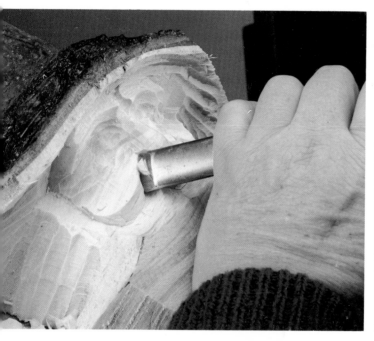

When you get near the back of the nostril turn the tool over so the cup side is against the work.

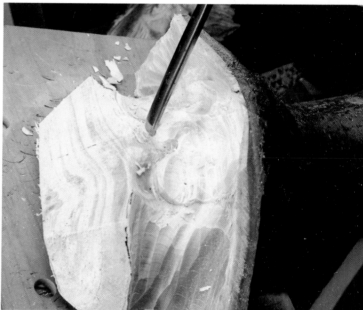

The middle of the underside of the nose is a little long, so I will come over it with the gouge, cup side against the nose.

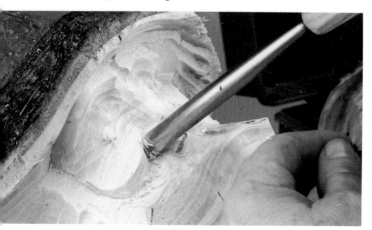

Find a half-round gouge that fits the nostril side and push it, cup side in, along the side of the nostril for a good smooth cut.

Progress.

Repeat on the other side.

Next, I need to define the moustache a little bit. I start with the bottom edge so I get some idea of what I have to play with.

Find a gouge that matches the curve of the moustache.

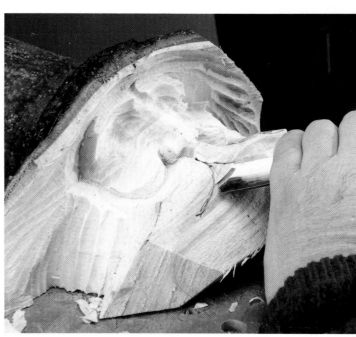

Clean out the area between the two sides of the moustache.

Drive it straight into the line for a stop.

Go back and repeat the process to deepen this area.

With a wide gouge work your way out from the center and reduce the beard area.

Progress.

Continue around the side.

Thin the moustache down a little. You don't want it to be too heavy.

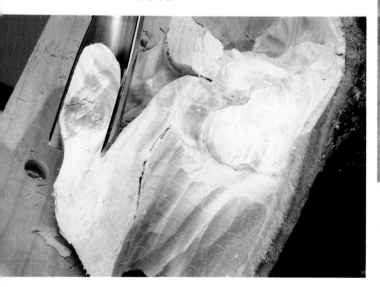

Turn the piece and repeat on the other side.

That takes you to this point.

Use a large v-tool to put some prominent lines under the moustache...

and over it. This brings it out dramatically.

Do the same on the other side.

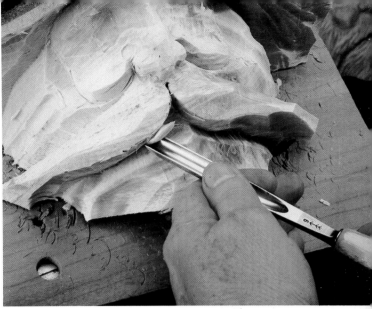

With a smaller half-round gouge work create the curve under the bottom lip by working from the center out.

Do the same thing where the hair meets the hat.

Crimp off the chip by pushing the skew straight in at the moustache line.

This adds some nice detail.

You want to establish some major beard lines using a small half-round gouge. The hairs radiate from the center, so you want to establish that line first. It should curve down from the lip and work its way to the chin.

You can add to this line if you want.

Then move to the other...

Other lines should go off to the side. Work on one side..

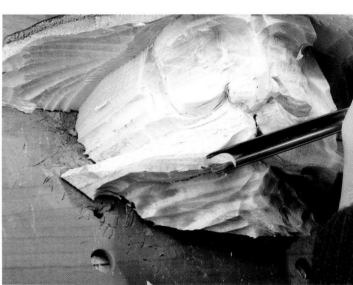

and do the same.

adding one or two lines.

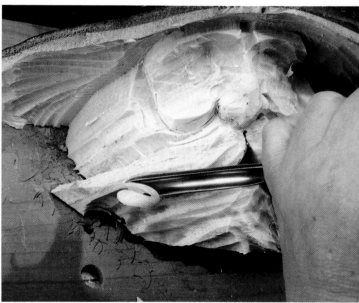

The same technique is used on the moustache with four or five lines from the center...

to establish the flow.

and the hair.

Continue the process into the hair. I'm doing this after just one side of the moustache is completed so I don't have to turn the piece as much.

Use a v-tool to sharpen the line between the brow and the hat.

Switch to the other side and do the moustache...

Soften the shape of the cheeks.

Straighten up the eyebrows.

Clean up the lines under the brim of the hat.

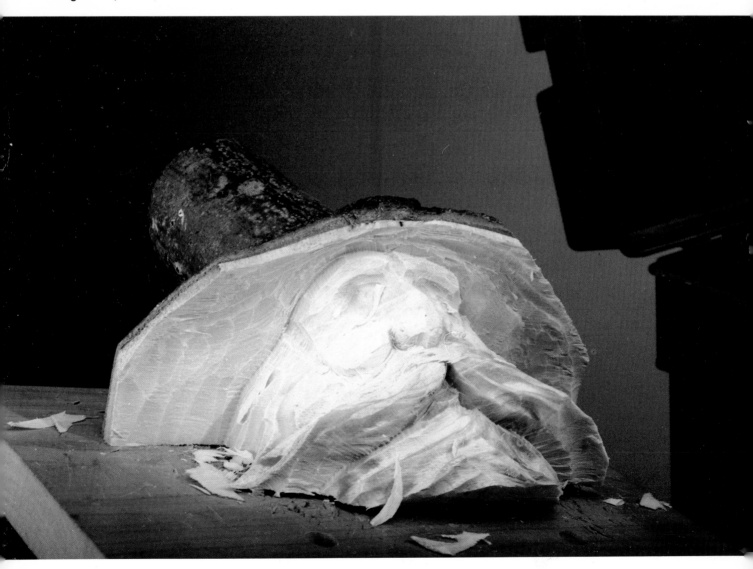

The smoothed brim.

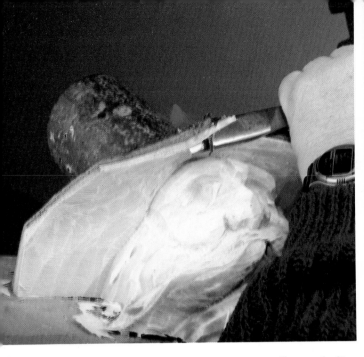

While you're in this position, you might as well round off the edge of the hat with the chisel.

Use the same chisel to make a line over the top of the brow.

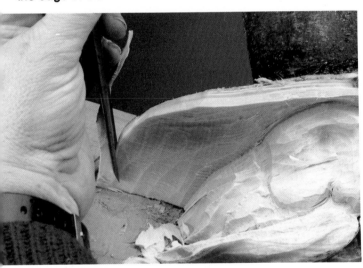

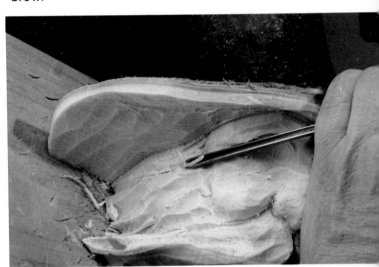

You'll want to curve it back at the ends.

Start creating hairs around the face.

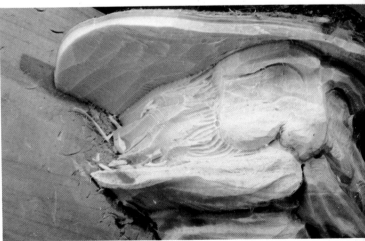

With a big veiner define the underside of the eyebrow.

Work your way down to the moustache.

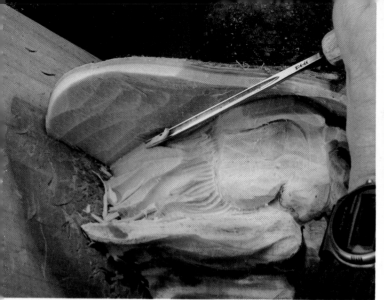

Follow some major lines. Keep them flowing nicely.

With a v-tool go up the line between the sides of the moustache. Be careful not to go into the nose.

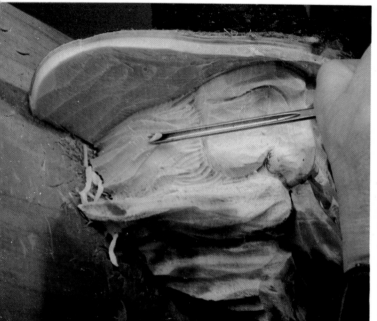

Work your way down the hairline.

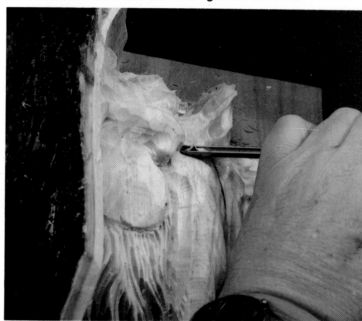

Begin the hairs of the moustache by going into the nose first.

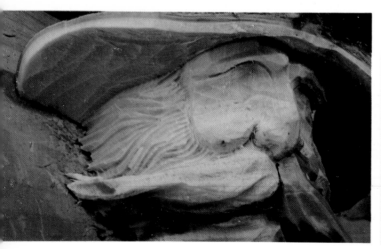

The hair on one side is done.

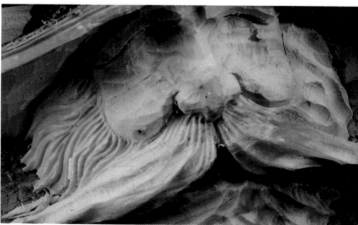

These early cuts help set the pattern.

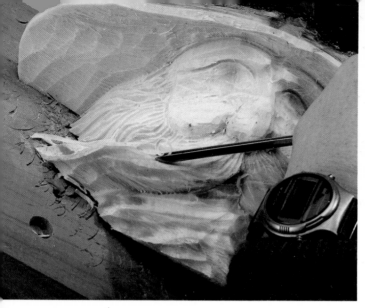

Bring the longer lines across...

Start with the hairs in the center.

and over the top to give the moustache character and depth.

Turn the piece and repeat the process.

Only the chin is left to go.

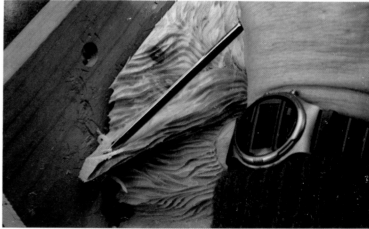

While the piece is in this position dress up the underside of the moustache.

To align the eyes, imagine 5 across. This will also help you spot mistakes in the facial balance, like here on the right side.

Trim the face with a gouge, first cutting straight in against the face...

then cutting under the brim...

Finally cut from the side burn.

Draw in the top line of the eye following the lines of the brow.

Go back and fix the hair line...

Add the lower line and the iris.

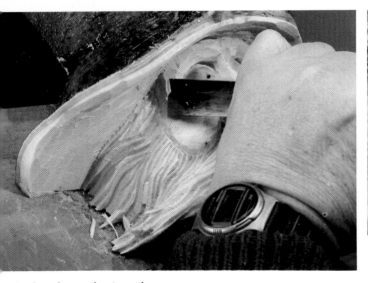

and reshape the temple.

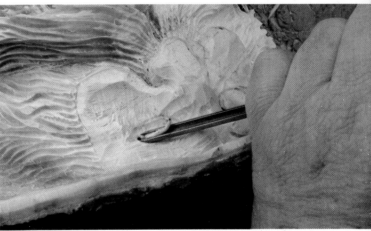

With a veiner go around the eyes. I do the figure's left eye first upside down, because it is less awkward this way. Do one line...

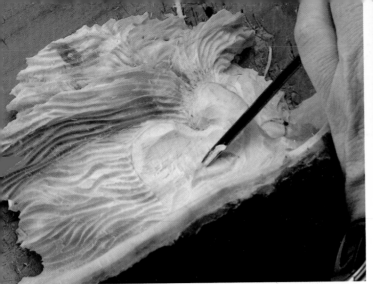

then the other.

In the outside corner of the eye use the skew to cut into the line of the top lid...

Turn the piece over and do its right eye in the same way, one side...

and the bottom lid.

then the other.

Then come across the plane of the eyeball and cut out the triangle.

The result.

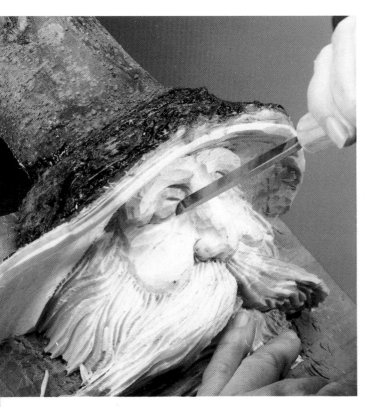

Repeat the process on the inside corner. Lower lid.

Upper lid.

Across the bottom.

Mark the crow's feet in the corners of the eyes and the bags under the eyes.

This eye is a little small, so I'll open it with a veiner.

Cut the line of the bag with the veiner held so one side is cutting into the wood more than the other.

Round the eyeball off with a skew.

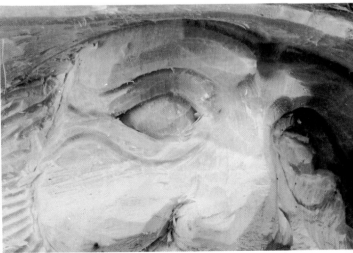

This gives the effect of it being bagged down.

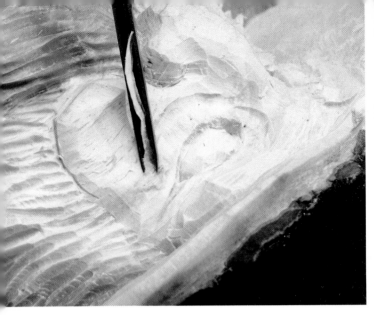

Do the same on the other side.

Deepen the line above the upper lid.

A small v-tool should give the sharp line we want for the crow's feet.

With a veiner add hair lines to the eyebrows, starting at the inside and working your way out.

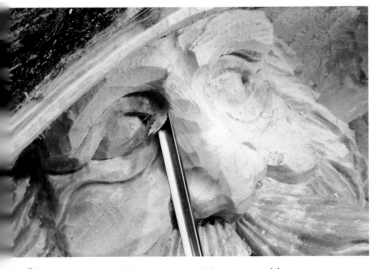

Clean out the inside corners of the eyes with a gouge.

The finished eyebrow.

The face. All it needs is a little cleaning.

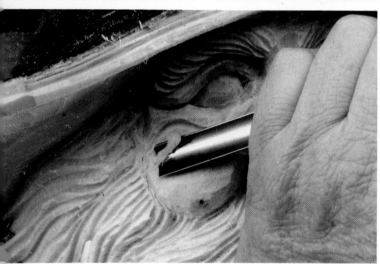

Use a gouge and carefully go over the rough spots of the cheeks.

Ready for painting.

34

Painting the Woodspirit

As you can see from the gallery, it is not necessary to paint Woodspirits. A natural finish is very effective. But when I do I use Winsor and Newton Alkyd tube paints. These are thinned with pure turpentine to a consistency that is soaked into the carving, giving subtle colors. What I look for is a watery mixture, almost like a wash. In this way the turpentine will carry the pigment into the wood, giving the stained look I like. It has always been my theory that if you are going to cover the wood, why use wood in the first place. It should be noted that with white, the concentration of the pigment should be a little stronger.

I mix my paints in juice bottles, putting in a bit of paint and adding turpentine. I don't use exact measurements. Instead I use trial and error, adding a bit of paint or a bit of turpentine until I get the thickness I want.

The juice bottles are handy for holding your paints. They are reclosable, easy to shake, and have the added advantage of leaving a concentrated amount of color on the inside of the lid and the sides of the bottle which can be used when more intense color is needed.

Prepare the piece for painting by rubbing it with turpentine. This will help make the waxy areas more receptive to the paint.

Paint the face with flesh tone paint. This is a mixture of tube flesh, white, and raw sienna.

Blend it out...

Put dots of red on the nose, cheeks, and lip.

to give a rosy hue to the skin.

Apply white to the eyes.

The hair will have an undercoat of yellow. I start at the hat...

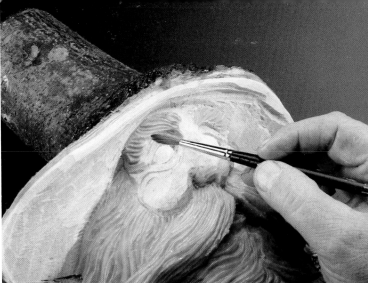

On the eyebrows, more or less dry brush the orange so it catches the ridges.

and work my way around.

Stain the underside of the brim with a light sienna paint.

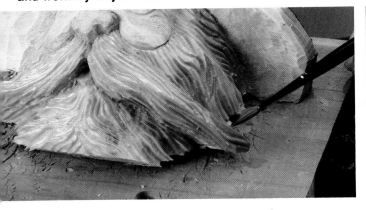

Blend in an overcoat of orange. Start with the strongest pigment at the extremities and spread it in toward the center. Of course, on another day I might do just the opposite.

The figure is looking up and slightly to the right, so I apply the blue irises in the appropriate areas.

Add the black of the pupil

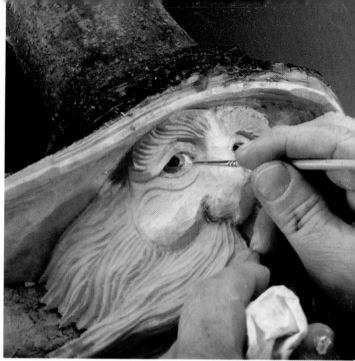

A glint of white gives the eyes life.

The painted woodspirit.

The Gallery